SECOND CHANCES

J. SAUNDERS

SECOND CHANCES

Copyright © Rad Press Publishing
J. Saunders
"Second Chances"

All rights reserved. No part of this publication
may be reproduced, distributed or conveyed
without the permission of the author.

J. SAUNDERS

There are too many people to thank and list when I consider my dedication page. For the ones who listened to me ramble and who let me type away on my phone in the middle of a conversation. The individuals who would receive random photos of my work as I wrote this... there's a solid four of you I owe a lot to. The Instagram community. For those who have been with me on this journey. The love and support. Thank you. Y.L, S.N, C.M, T.G, B.T, T.T, my ma but most importantly my king, F. Saunders, everything I do is for you.

SECOND CHANCES

This book is my journey. From the past to the present. Who I was and who I became. The beginning of my story isn't the most pleasant, be warned but it's not the past that matters, it's where you're headed. If you find yourself within my words from pain, I send you my love. I encourage you to read this journey to the end. Light your pathway or it will forever be dark. The road of self-love is never ending, never give up. Nothing in life matters if you are not happy. Do not be oblivious to your needs. Finally, I hope you believe in second chances when everything around you suggest- ed you were not good enough.

HOW IT WAS

I was a woman trapped in a cage by a man who didn't love me.
He left me with no pages or ink to express my state of mind,
knowing I'd write about him and all his false promises.

SECOND CHANCES

DREAMS

It's never a time and a place,
a sign or a notion from the universe.
Usually it's sheer gut and determination
to accomplish all the dreams you've
kept locked away.

Hemingway once wrote, "Write hard and clear about what hurts.", So I did.

SECOND CHANCES

HOW IT WENT

There are just certain places you can't go to after a break
up. The same way you can't listen to certain songs
anymore, they just hit too deep.
Places and music remind me of the women you wanted
over me. Daily, you threw other people's words of love
at my heart as if it never mattered.
Breaking up with a woman who wasn't even yours,
had you running home crying,
to the only one who truly loved you.

It hurts to know
that at one point
I was everything to you.
The sky didn't seem untouchable.
Heart didn't seem breakable.

It's hard to swallow reality when
you woke up one day
and I was no longer good enough.

SECOND CHANCES

LOVE AFFAIR

You slowly unzip my dress while
standing behind me, moving
my hair to the side. Exposing
my freckled bare skin,
removing the straps holding up my silk dress,
now watching it fall to the floor.
Hands touching my thighs,
reaching up to cusp my breasts,
gently kissing my shoulders before I turn around.
Hands behind my back.
Lips pressed into mine.
I indulge in our passion.

What happened?
We were so good just now.

                                                        I know, I'm sorry.
                            I just have this thing with my neck...
                                  you grabbed it and I panicked.

                            Here's a tissue your nose is bleeding.

Do we need to talk about it?

                                                      There is nothing to say.

            I didn't know where to start

SECOND CHANCES

BEFORE TODAY

I don't think it's possible to forget the look on your fathers face when he called out and I emerged. He looked at me and his face filled with sorrow. He could tell I had been crying, eyes swollen, face and neck red. We stared at each other for a minute before his voice cracked, telling me he'd bring me home. He stood up and took a step towards his son, I turned and grabbed my jacket. The car ride was silent. We live four major intersections apart but the roads in Toronto are long and this car ride felt like a plane flight. He pulled up to the back door of my building and turned around in his seat. He just kept staring, unsure of what to say and to be honest I don't blame him. I said, "thank you for the ride home" and got out of the car.

I'll never understand what
ran through your mind
when shoving me onto the bed,
opening my legs,
hand gripping my neck,
forcing my face into the sheets
seemed normal to you.

I didn't ask you to touch me
betray my trust and spread my legs,
so you could violate me.

You took my innocence,
my purity and tainted me.

No one deserves things to be taken
without permission.

10 years later,
I still take multiple showers a day,
then ask why.

SECOND CHANCES

CALVINGTON

"These roads don't lead
to my home,
why are you turning here?".

"Relax" he said,
as we pulled onto a dead-end street,
the other side of my middle school.

Hill top he leans over and says,
"your ex was Greek right?
Your girlfriend told me,
which means,
you should know what we like.",
while unzipping his pants
gripping the roots of my hair,
palm against my skull.

J. SAUNDERS

I knew, he had an alternative motive. Somewhere inside I ignored my gut because I've always wanted to believe the better in people.

SECOND CHANCES

YOU CAN TRUST ME 2.0

We were friends
until a few drinks later
and I'm your prey.
Waking up to your movements
holding my body from falling,
while you take me from behind.
My memory is impeccable...
except that night is a blur,
I am unable to recall how or why.
Just aware that you took advantage.

J. SAUNDERS

I remember speaking so highly of you,
Introducing you to my friends.
Gave you the trust I figured you earned,
and you ruined it when I was unstable.
Taking advantage of me that spring evening.

SECOND CHANCES

PICK A YEAR AND A SEASON

It didn't matter how many times I said no,
nothing could change your weight, nor force on top of me.
Zippers are breakable.
Fabric can be ripped.
Small wrists in a large grip.
With every chance to fight,
I lost strength in each no I breathed.

J. SAUNDERS

I want to rip your heart from your chest,
place it in the palm of my hand
and squeeze it, till I feel little to no pulse left.
My nails digging into the sides,
blood leaking through the cracks of my fingers.
Only to give it back,
damaged and full of pain,
unable to stop screaming my name.

Take an Advil, the screams get louder.

FIRST RELATIONSHIP

I am human.
A woman you mistreated
like unwanted property.
Abusing me
till I was too damaged
to withstand my own weight.
Left on the floor,
shoved under a bed
alone in an unfamiliar place,
suffering from what I thought was love.

J. SAUNDERS

I have run out of excuses
when people ask me why
my face is tainted
from the force of a man's hand,
putting his lips in places
he was not invited to.

SECOND CHANCES

I know it's going to be okay
for right now,
let me be.

I want to understand my pain.

KARMA BEGINS

I secretly rejoice the night you called me drunk.
You had fallen and
unsure how to get home,
asking me to pick you up at 3 am.

I vividly remember telling you to call *her*,
and you said, you did already.

I hung up.

Neither of the women you epically played cared enough
to get you in your drunken state,
because she was at home with her new man
and I was over you.

SECOND CHANCES

EMBARRASSED

I'm no longer disappointed
in myself for loving you.
However, I'm angry with you
for allowing this charade to go on,
when you had no intention on loving me.

Titles are overrated.
You weren't my fiancé.
You were the "love of my life",
and you destroyed everything
a woman could dream of.

SECOND CHANCES

No words are left to describe the way I loved you.
You learned that It's true,
you never know what you have till it's gone.
I gave you years of my life that I'll never get back
just to help you build yours.
To give you love and a happy home.
I need you to understand that my book is written in a past tense.

It was then when I loved you.
Today, you're one out of over a billion people.
You became the masses.

Did I ever really love you
or did I love everything I thought
we were supposed to be,
while holding onto false hope?

These are my questions.

SECOND CHANCES

You promised me love.

Giving me everything but that.

J. SAUNDERS

I imagine my life before you,
then shake my head in disbelief.
Now knowing how much one person
can truly impact your life.

SECOND CHANCES

You're only hurting them.
The women you're sleeping with,
because of the void you feel since I left.
You could fuck the life out of their souls
and still not win their hearts.

You're only hurting them.
The women you leave after searching for me,
with no satisfaction.

I loved you more than you'll ever know.
More than your wildest dreams.
I loved you so much that when you left
there was still leftover love within me.

SECOND CHANCES

TODAY'S THOUGHT

I don't recall love anymore.
I only know the low blows
of my painful past
as daily reminders in my office space.

WALLS

It wasn't always so bad, why can't we make this work?
Make us whole, be together again?

For every time you missed my face.

For every fight that lead you to throwing objects,
punching walls.
I covered each unfilled hole with a butterfly photo.

We fought so often,
the walls were filled.

They were a daily reminder of my prison,
until I set myself free from waking up to an empty bed
and walls not decorated with love.

This is my response to your unanswered questions.

SECOND CHANCES

Had I known your understanding of jewelry
was your fingerprints in black and blue
along my pale skin,
I would have thought twice before devoting myself to you.

My love was not meant to be caged by the arms of a man who tried to control it.

SECOND CHANCES

The word love is over played and over used, but it's the best four letters I have left to use against him.

Lickspittle, Ottomy, Vain-glorious, Eye-sore.

J. SAUNDERS

I used to pray,
I'd be the one
who'd make you laugh
for the rest of your life
until you muted me.

Delivering a single rose
each day,
from the dozen
you had given to her.

SECOND CHANCES

I loved you with every atom in my body.
Loved you from places in my soul
I never knew existed,
and instead of loving me back,
you made my body your place of
bruised damaged art,
before suggesting I wear a sweater dress
and skip lunch.

Love, like us, shouldn't be tucked away and spoken as a memory
but that is all that we are now.

SECOND CHANCES

If I could go back in time
the only thing I would change
is how I treated you.

I gave you too much of me,
and you had too much control.

There is a vast difference
between being alone and being lonely.
These days I am alone,
but I knew loneliness when I was with you.

SECOND CHANCES

wicked
cruel
reckless
savage
ruthless
demon

                                                          crystallized
                                                                 angel
                                                             captured
                                                                  wings
                                                               clipped
                                                          irretrievable

relentless
silver
gun
amusement
roulette

J. SAUNDERS

I secretly hope you're suffering.
I don't wish illness on anyone.
Instead I wish them well.
But if I could have one wish for you,
knowing I'm worse,
than my worst enemy
it would be addiction.
Addiction to self-inflicted pain,
caused by each thought of me.
Every memory and emotion of yearning,
you suffer over and over.

SECOND CHANCES

Sometimes I miss it,
the pretending,
the people who used to surround me.
I wonder if life was easier than
verse now,
knowing people prefer the lies
over the truth any day.

I am full of excuses
Like excusing your promises
when you vowed to love me

SECOND CHANCES

Maybe one day I'll stop writing about Peter Pan
dressed as a man.

Not today,
but maybe tomorrow.

WAR OF LOVE

We were crazy.
He was psychotic.
I was mad.
I am nowhere near innocent
when it comes to our relationship,
although I never deserved the violence;
I have a spiteful tongue
when releasing all the pain I've held onto.
Empty threats and empty bullet chambers,
but his were always full.
Neither of us were perfect.
Our relationship was like a ticking time bomb
always on the defense,
because I couldn't trust him,
and he couldn't be honest.

SECOND CHANCES

> I broke up with you
> But you left me
> in the ruins of my own home,

it was a fake forever after.

J. SAUNDERS

MAN OF LIES

You played me like a piano,
hitting all the right keys
as if it was the song to my heart.

You never knew my favourite flower
So, you'd play the violin whenever I was upset,
distracting my mind before taking control.

SECOND CHANCES

I loved you
        with each thought that came to mind,
   with each beat my heart would take,
with every cell in my body,
I loved you,
but that
      was
          then.

Vile romance triggered a version of a woman I never knew.
Who was she and why did she love you, while loathing
herself?

SECOND CHANCES

What about us?

You left remember?

~~Something~~
Someone else was more important
and you came back different.

It took another woman,
for you to realize my value.

Did she not cook like me?
Did she not communicate like me?
Treat you like a king, like I was?
Did she not love and make love to you...
like I did?

Like. I. Did.

I loved you

now

my heart hurts.

This would be considered normal
if you hadn't stuck around
after discovering I loved you,
knowing you'd never love me back.

SECOND CHANCES

ONLY IF

While winging my eyeliner in the car mirror
as people hustle into the back seats
violently a woman taps on my window
and says,
"just because you get picked up first,
doesn't mean you get to sit in the front.
Next time I ride shot gun.".

You sat in the driver's seat
unable to say a word to me.
I laughed and thought,
if she only knew.

If she only knew,
the car was mine.
I tucked you in the night before
and made you breakfast in the morning.
Only if she knew,
getting picked up first doesn't match,
your fiancés description,
when you lock the front door behind me.
Only if she knew,
you're a pathological liar,
and without me in the background
building your dreams,
she wouldn't have looked at you.

I think back and wonder,
how and why I managed to suffer.
To wake up and do it all again.
Smile during the day,
fearing for the closed doors at night.
Being with you was life's lesson,
on how to self-destruct.

She called me long distance one day,
to apologize. She didn't know, but I did.

J. SAUNDERS

You were too busy letting me down
that when I left
you had the nerve to ask why.

SECOND CHANCES

My biggest fear is running out of words and having to face my heart. I would rather my mind tell me stories about our love than deal with immense emotions I've contained.

J. SAUNDERS

Don't you get it?
Or are you that self-centered?
That narcissistic?
Fact that, I was too tall for you,
so you'd knock me down,
while your height averaged 5'11,
my 8-inch difference in shortness
was based on my efforts in life
where you slacked.

You broke my soul,
every time you had a chance.
Your bare hands wrapped around
my arms pinning me down,
in all the wrong ways,
unable to break free;
before you'd press your
lips against mine,
after threats and disgrace
were slapped on me.

When my soft voice
was barely heard
but my mind was screaming.
It must have rippled through,
when you snapped that night,
and missed my jawline
that poor wall. All four walls,
were demolished by
the time I left.
Four walls;
literally, my home,
and comparatively, my heart.

SECOND CHANCES

You were so caught up
with lust,
you'd rip my clothes off without
truly looking at me.
Caught up with greed;
a hard-working woman,
supporting you and your women.
Caught up with rage;
angry how another woman
did you wrong...
so, you did worse to me,
as if I wasn't worthy of love.

I am worthy.

J. SAUNDERS

We had good moments,
loud laughs,
nice memories,
but I have more pain,
than love,
when I reminisce about us.

SECOND CHANCES

PUERTO RICO

Although the sunset reminds me,
it is, you who I want.
It is, you who I love.
You've done nothing but hurt me.
As I sit on this shoreline
I reflect knowing this is where I belong,
however, I question if I belong here with you,
or do I belong with someone else.

J. SAUNDERS

You were my first love and love,
you were ruthless.

You were a savage,
and shattered me to pieces.

Mentally, emotionally and physically
you ruined me.

I was the smallest woman alive
when I was with you.

SECOND CHANCES

What did you expect from a woman whose words
only came from the ink of a pen? Your name written with hearts for
I's? With X's and O's beside it? I recall the same hands holding this
book were once around my neck. I remember, you being my biggest
supporter, to my greatest enemy.

WHO DO YOU THINK YOU ARE?

You don't get to run around
ruining other people,
just because the person
you proclaimed to love,
ruined you.
It doesn't work that way.
Go home and fix yourself.

Do not go putting your toxic hands on pure souls.

SECOND CHANCES

I need you to understand
that it is not easy to trust a man
who says, my hands will give you love,
my arms will hold you for protection,
spend the night and let me wake up to you;
when men before him,
said similar words
and caused damage instead.

I know long shirts from bruises and heartache
from a deceiver who enjoyed other women.
Trust is something I no longer
give away for free.

J. SAUNDERS

I long to express
the grief which lays within my heart,
that trickles down into my soul
darkening with each drop
my heart bleeds of pain

SECOND CHANCES

I thought rock bottom was the months to follow our break up and your stalking. A year it took before you stopped putting unwanted letters in my window. I used to park at my boyfriend's place a year and a half later standing on the veranda, wondering if you were going to turn the corner, because you had a tracker in my car. I asked you to leave the city because no matter how far I truly was in distance, you were always that type of person who'd find a way to capture me. Rock bottom was years later when you finally gave up.

J. SAUNDERS

You came looking for it and found nothing.
You pushed my mother out of the way
and entered a space that you were not invited to.
Trespasser.

It was never yours
and your heart was never mine.
The key is.

I'll wear its diamonds if I want to.

BUSINESS ARRANGEMENT

He would kiss the rock on my finger
and vow to love me.

He stopped providing love to my heart
but loved the material things
holding us together.

I write about the way love betrayed me
because all I ever did was believe in it.

SECOND CHANCES

FIGHT NIGHT

Love is not a constant fight,
if I must fight to get you,
I'll have to fight to keep you.
Fight myself into happiness when you're mad,
sleeping in the other room
after another fight,
both questioning why.
I may never know
what love truly is,
but I doubt it's anything
I just described.

J. SAUNDERS

I want you to call me.
I want to see your name light up on my phone,
hear your voice when you say "hello".
I want to submerge into your tone
when you say, I miss you;
to have a momentary pause
then say,
I missed you,
before hanging up.

SECOND CHANCES

Sometimes,
it was over nothing.
Few times,
we had our reasons.
Many times,
our screams were so loud
we couldn't hear each other.
We often forgot how we got to that point.

Many times;
a few times,
sometimes,
he'd use his hands
to stop my screams
just to hear himself.

J. SAUNDERS

It was a lie.
you were a lie,
the manufacturer.
I lost my mind
when the home of my heart
fell apart
from your betrayal.

SECOND CHANCES

Be mindful of their words.

The ones who listen the most,
also know the right things to say,
just to get their way.

When I'm no longer missing you.
When I'm over those nights
staying up analyzing
our last conversation together.
When I'm over replaying our memories
between the good and the great,
you're going to wish
I still missed you.
When missing you is no longer an option,
you're going to feel it.
Feel it in the center of your entire existence,
me, moving on from you,
I hope it hurts.

SECOND CHANCES

SAFE NOW

27,458 tally marks
counting the amount of times
I thought about suicide when I was with you
before passing out.

42,986 tally marks
counting the amount of times
I thought about suicide caused by fear of you
before telling myself,
I was going to be okay.

J. SAUNDERS

Be passionate

Be proactive

Be patient

with yourself

SECOND CHANCES

Someone will hurt you at least once in your life. No matter what you do; how hard you try to avoid it from happening, someone is going to try and ruin you. Rip you to pieces and break you down. In this process you'll learn just how strong you are. Just how important it is to love yourself and know, that you can conquer anything and anyone, when you're over being on the floor.

You deserve everything this world has to offer.

You deserve to laugh, and you deserve to be loved.

Do not rely on someone else to provide what you're deserving of.

Happiness is deserved from within, not another human.

You deserve flowers and kisses at every hour.

You deserve stargazing and adventures.

I beg you to never settle.

SECOND CHANCES

Unfolding in the cracks of our love
you can find habits which are no longer ours,
but yours and mine
pulling apart the trivial things
that once brought us so close together.

You could've taken the rest of my pride,
taken the remaining money in my accounts;
destroyed my car,
tell me,
you never loved me,
this was all just a game.
You could've cut off my hands,
left me naked in the middle of no-where,
you could've done anything,
except take my poetry.

You did everything in your power
to stop me from writing.
You hated when I tuned you out,
just to write, dear diary.

You had no right to open the pages of my work.
The countless pages of my unspoken words
after muting me.
You had no right to write a note in an unwritten journal,
asking for forgiveness;
writing you loved me,
how sorry you were,
for not noticing all the pain I was in
because pill popping and
not eating, wasn't obvious enough.

You took my poetry.
You took everything from me.
Those poems meant more to me
than my love for you ever will.

SECOND CHANCES

While we were playing
house, he was building one
for her

J. SAUNDERS

I am going insane
as my heart searches for home.
Like a rose with a thorn,
I bleed with the love he claims to give me.

SECOND CHANCES

BEFORE YESTERDAY

I had no idea who I was.
desperately I needed you.
Stripping me of everything and everyone
I once knew.
Thus, becoming a figment of my imagination,
I was mentally unstable.
Unable to pull myself away
from the devil's grip.
Until the Lord, heard my screams
and saved me.
Yesterday was the last day
of the old me.

J. SAUNDERS

Our biggest problem
was you holding the gun
shooting rounds for days
then acting like the victim.

SECOND CHANCES

6 YEARS LATER

They say,
eventually you forget about the love you once had.
Someone will ask you their favourite sports team or colour,
and you'll hesitate.
I disagree but maybe that's just me.
Because I can recall your favourite team and colour.
I can recall your favourite meal and the dreams you'd
constantly talk about until 3 am.
These must be my consequences for loving you.
Knowing you'll hesitate if someone asks you about mine.

J. SAUNDERS

I fell for your games
like I was Jenga.
Brick by brick,
I fell.

SECOND CHANCES

There was a time when
we were full of love and desire,
though our fire was dying.
We'd walk down the streets
of Old Forest Hill building our dream home,
discussing anything that didn't make us angry.
I know you think I got tired of it.
Truthfully, I loathed it.
All I ever wanted was you.
Another set of four walls,
titled home wouldn't have changed
the road we were about to walk down.
Hands no longer intertwined
creating space where our love fell
sadly remaining on the pathways, I no longer visit.

- All I wanted was you and all you wanted was the dream.

J. SAUNDERS

I wasn't always a bitter, broken woman.
Imagine peach skies;
clear oceans,
white sand.
That spell that makes you feel alive.
The honey moon stage lasting beyond days and months,
then the one you're going to spend your life with
leaves your flower filled castle for another.
Thus, turning it into
red skies;
blood water,
black sand.
Rips the haze from your heart,
turns your blue eyes to grey.

You see,
I knew love and
the war for love too.
Despite winning the battle,
my prince still betrayed me
so, fuck ever after.

SECOND CHANCES

Too short.
Heals too high.
Long hair.
Never short.
Never blonde.
Make-up.
Outfits set.
Too fat.
Too skinny.
Very sexual.
Loss of interest.
Hates silence.
Talk too much.
All I read.
Are the shots.
You took at me.
While screaming:
be happy,
smile more,
I love you.
But never satisfied.
Never were
you happy
or in love
with me.

It was a bad idea to love you.
I'll never be able to wrap my mind around her words.
He asked me if there was a future for us,
if not, he was going to ask you to marry him.

I lost my mind that night,
and you can tell me you had the ring.
You can tell me every lie in the book,
but we both know you would've died for her
yet still never had her heart.

I am not a backup plan,
but to you I was.

SECOND CHANCES

I didn't expect or want this.

I didn't just wake up one morning and say,
"fuck this, I deserve better",
then got up and left.

No.

I spent years allowing you to belittle me into a corner,
then let you put a cape on and save me.

It was a vicious cycle.

It was unhealthy and unnatural.

I woke up one morning,
learning how blind I was from love.

Loving someone else just isn't enough
when you've been unloved for just as long.

There were many unfortunate
reasons why we ended,
but the nights I fell asleep alone
with you in our home
to wake up without you,
is the biggest one for me.

SECOND CHANCES

We fought so often
that not fighting became a high-five.
Insomnia and I were always friends,
but our friendship grew
the night your hand met my neck,
smashing my head into the headboard
of our bed.
I stayed up, night after night tracing
my finger over the dent debating
how I should get you back.

- All I have are my words

Every once and awhile he'd pick up the phone and call me.
Shoot me a text to let me know he was thinking of me.   Just
a reminder of, "remember when? It wasn't always ugly.
We had some good times,
some great moments.".

I used to think he had trouble letting go
but in truth, he was looking for closure...
and every once and awhile,
I'd reply with a brief "thank you,
hope you're well too".

Eventually, the replies stopped.
I didn't have the heart to ask him to stop messaging me.
He was looking for something I couldn't provide,
after years of giving him everything I could.

SECOND CHANCES

THANKFUL

Between the highs and the lows
of everything we were;
I needed you to give me,
show me all that you had
or therefore lack of,
to understand that
love is everything you were not.
Everything we were not.
This taught me.
Flourished me to know
better for next time.

J. SAUNDERS

I never told you
that when I walked away from you,
I dropped my heart on the ground
because it was filled with unwavering love for you.
I was unable to relieve it,
unable to let go.
And I never told you
the way I've missed you,
is more than the way I loved you
no other woman will be able to compare.

SECOND CHANCES

I never asked you for anything.
Maybe that was my problem,
you left me with literally nothing.
Confused when I asked you, why?
After years of you continuously being here
with no expectations.

J. SAUNDERS

Your love still takes shots at me whenever
I see you standing in the space
I was supposed to call my own.
Constantly, I am torn between
being okay and moved on, to falling
apart and cursing your name.

SECOND CHANCES

I don't want your pity apology.
You made all those people
think you're sorry,
but I don't believe you,
nor do I forgive you.

J. SAUNDERS

LETYOUKNOW

I was madly in love with you.
I was also blind and deaf to reality.

Finally, after the last time you hit me
and threw me onto the street from my own vehicle -

No

Finally, after her and I discussed the relationship the two of
you had. The one you came home "broken" over.
Crawling into bed beside me, asking me to tend to your
pathetic needs because it was over between you two.

No

Finally, after you accused me of cheating on you with
someone, simply because I sat in the same row as them -

No

Honestly, that wasn't it either.
I'm sure, I'll narrow it down one day and let you
know why I left you.

SECOND CHANCES

I needed you
to make mistakes.
To live, learn and love all the wrong things,
including you.

I discovered not only
how I deserve to be loved.
I discovered how to love, support and trust myself,
when you were unable to step up
and be the man I thought you were.

J. SAUNDERS

I think,
we were young.
We must have been foolish
thinking we were in love.

Truthfully,
I tell myself that sometimes
because the psychological abuse card
is still used in my everyday life.
Men meet me and know,
someone has hurt me.

Unable to speak for us,
but I loved.
I loved so much that I gave
everything up and myself away.
I was manipulated into thinking
there was nowhere,
and no one else for me.

We were young.
Fools to think,
we were in love.

SECOND CHANCES

BEGINNING TO END

I was the butterfly you loved at first sight,
catching your eyes attention as I fluttered by.
You captured me to take me home and keep me;
admire me,
love me,
but your hands where too tight
and I'm a restless type.
Indifferences removed the dust from my wings,
I no longer had the ability to flutter
as your heart desired.

You made a mess of my heart.
It wasn't okay then,
but it is now.
I survived what I thought
was an unmanageable catastrophe,
and after cleaning up pieces of myself
I realized, I never needed you.
You're not wanted here
unless you want your heart
on the floor in my possession.
I walk around in black leather lingerie,
and thigh high heels.
I am bold.
I am confident.
I am adequate.
Everything you hate.
Wearing nothing for you to grab
I know your tricks now.
Gun and knife holstered on my thigh,
at hands reach for the day you try
and break down my door.

Welcome home honey.

SECOND CHANCES

It took me a few years to realize
how dumb I was for letting you have the ability
in deciding what career was meant for me.
I've always been good at business,
I built one, twice on your behalf.
After you let success
slip through your fingers.
It's my turn now.
This is my world.
I suggest you step out while you still can.

I prefer to love someone with a deep soul.

Someone who is worthy and who doesn't make me feel
like I am ever a hard woman to love.

I know I am not perfect,
but I believe in the dusk before dawn.
Wishes at 11:11 and love at first sight.

Someone who'll love me
after conversations till 4 am,
when the sun rises
doesn't seem like too much to ask for.

SECOND CHANCES

She didn't want the typical rain storms.
Her love is as deep as the ocean.
She wanted a hurricane.
Someone to wrap a tornado around her heart
because she deserved that.

J. SAUNDERS

SECOND CHANCES

SECOND LOVE

As I take off my shirt
I love when your teeth graze my breast,
then biting my ribs,
kissing my lips,
lifting me above your head,
my legs wrapping around your body,
your eyes staring into mine.

I laugh
while you grin and throw me over your shoulders,
carrying me up the stairs
and we both know
you're going to throw me onto the bed...

I digress,
it's been years
but it feels like yesterday.

Somehow, I lost myself.
Lost in you.
Somewhere, between
the midnight affairs
and morning coffee.

N E W R O M A N C E

I can feel it, every
fiber in me.

Love

If you want to steal my heart
I won't put up a fight.

You can have it.

LIBRA'S

Laying in bed naked he would trace his fingers along my back.
Making unknown designs and marks while telling a story.
Chuckling each time before saying,
he was creating fairy tales of him and I,
with the freckles on my back.
Before kissing the freckles in places no one could see.

SECOND CHANCES

He pushed my hair
past my shoulder
and traced my tattoo
with his fingers.

His voice in my ear
that quiet evening
reading the words along my skin.

Still sends shivers
down my spine.

J. SAUNDERS

LOST LOVE

I met you,
fell in love
and was unable
to express the emotions
I felt within.

Only to lose you
because it was
too painful to love you
in silence.

SECOND CHANCES

LOVERNOTLOVE

I was lost in lust over you, but the haze eventually faded. I suddenly, was too much of a woman than you were willing to handle, all because I was worth more than the cheap nights you provided after tearing apart the concept of love.

ADDICTED

I remembered when he inhaled my senses,
putting his lips against my neck
through deep breaths
tearing my dress off,
telling me
I was more addictive than cocaine.

SECOND CHANCES

I was being selfish, but I couldn't help it.
I've thought about you before,
but never like this.

I've written about you before,
but never with words like this.

I've always wanted you.

Yet, never like how I want you right now,
without any interruptions.

But what if it's supposed to be us?
Between all the people and places,
we've crossed, we found each other.
We keep pushing the idea of love away
because of old faces and hurtful places.

What if we were the matching pair?
Speaking in past references from our memories
because we no longer believed in magic.
Instead we're left with imprints of our touch
that can't be erased and no other can match.

CONNECTED

I don't need you
but I'm emotionally attached.
I need you to stay
for my sanity.

SECOND CHANCES

WHAT MY HEART WANTS

Since I met you and had you.
Now that I know you exist.
There's nothing I can do
but wait for you.

J. SAUNDERS

I know you would've and could've.
I know you thought about it
but then something came up.

I know you say it's not intentional.

I know it's the cycle
and when you're ready
you'll be here.

You know
I just want to scream,
reach out to you,
hold you.

We know,
It's a waiting game
and I grow restless
waiting on you.

SECOND CHANCES

Your hands on my body
created a story
I would rewrite every day,
just to have you with me.

J. SAUNDERS

PLEASE DON'T LEAVE

In the places that
were unfilled
and damaged before
you came around,
demolishing my walls,
promising me love...
there are now flowers
I do not know
how to maintain.

SECOND CHANCES

I never understood how two people
so good for each other
run away from love,
and blame time for their encounter.

J. SAUNDERS

You knew all along
that they weren't the one for you,
but you waited around
holding onto unfinished conversations,
hoping that one day over a cup of coffee
while the sun rises
you'd be finishing them.

SECOND CHANCES

ONE- SIDED CONVERSATION WITH MY HEART

We can do this daily,
he is not coming back.

If you want to cry,
then cry.

You are entitled to your feelings.

I just need you to understand
that if he wanted to be with you,
he would.

If he wanted it to be,
it would be.

Love isn't indecisive.
Love may take time, work and sacrifice
but you're never unsure.
You simply know.

GREEK WARRIOR

You came to me
shattered and lonely
desperate to escape
what you knew.

I was fresh,
nothing like what
you had tasted before.

Thus, draining me
until you were bored.

J. SAUNDERS

The taste of you lingers on my lips,
tracing my skin where your hands used to touch,
I search for your lust with my fingertips.

Reminiscing on our long days,
late nights, all the loving and fucking,
those bittersweet memories.

This is where I can find you
exactly how you would leave me,
satisfied but lonely.

SECOND CHANCES

BREAK UP

Slowly, I am going to pull you apart
then put you back together with my love.

I'm in too deep
with the sound of ice shuffling
in another glass of Whiskey,
while the vinyl is on repeat.

SECOND CHANCES

These are the sleepless nights I warn you about,
where I'm tired but restless and unable to sleep,
wondering if there is something to write,
something to do.
Oh, what did I forget?
Then wishing you weren't necessarily here with me
but here in general
and *I miss you* aren't the words I'm looking for.
I have none, only this space.
This void I'm unable to fill on the moments you disappear
after you insinuated for me to wait,
keep myself available,
you'd be back.
Although you always return,
a piece of me has left.
Each time, there is less of the woman
you asked to wait for you.
I'm finding it harder...
pretending to be her.

J. SAUNDERS

Being with me was everything you thought you
never wanted.
I put you against the grain,
you wanted to change your ways,
your goals and dreams.
Suddenly, being with me wasn't just a one-night stand,
I was more than a lover and a friend.
Your heart told you this
but your past mistakes lead us to fall apart
when you couldn't commit to giving love a chance again.

SECOND CHANCES

My love is soul deep,
inside out.

Your love is superficial,
surface based.

That's our difference,
that's why
we never worked.

Don't do that
Don't touch me like I am yours
then leave me like I am someone else's.

Don't do that
I am not a cheap love affair
for you to love when it's convenient for you.

Don't do that
Do not have an empty conversation about what ifs
when you have no intentions on staying.

SECOND CHANCES

HE WAS TEMPORARY

I told myself
when we were over
not to fall apart, but
I couldn't help it
With no self-control
I broke down,
lifeless and unable to move
I was a spitting image of sleeping beauty
You were in my dreams

J. SAUNDERS

It's okay to enjoy their company,
fall in love if you want too.
Never lose yourself in the unknown
unless it's within yourself.

SECOND CHANCES

RECENT LOVER

I fell to my knees,
losing you was a tragedy to me.
I did, I fell in love with you
now scared of my own reflection.
I hold myself and think back
to all the moments I wish
I could have had more time.

J. SAUNDERS

You're amongst the stars.
I can see you.
Unable to have you.
Asking the moon,
how you are.

SECOND CHANCES

Love was when
~~your happiness was mine.~~

Love was when
<u>I was with you.</u>

- Cliché of true facts

J. SAUNDERS

I wasn't aware
my heart needed insurance.
Was it theft or property damage
That I need to report since meeting you?

SECOND CHANCES

All I could do was cry
for hours,
days,
weeks.
Countless tears over you.

J. SAUNDERS

It'll be on a Sunday night when you decide,
that you've had enough of the taste of me.

A shot of Bourbon,
but I still exist.

Couple more,
before draining the bottle,
but I still exist.

Now you're drunk with regret,
knowing not only will you never forget me;
your heart will miss me,
your mind will replay me,
your hands will crave me.

I still exist,
far beyond your lips.

I am,
what you taste now.

SECOND CHANCES

I poured my heart out
and you took
my living beating organ,
as if it was nothing -
it meant, nothing.

Throwing it on the ground
watching you walk away,
as if I was nothing -
I meant - nothing.

J. SAUNDERS

You had me in the palm of your hand

till you pushed me off the edge of your fingertips

and now you've lost me.

SECOND CHANCES

...if actions speak louder than words
why do yours hurt so much?

I am breaking myself inside by sticking around
because I am unable to detach myself from loving you.

Who knew that caring about someone could become so suicidal.

SECOND CHANCES

I must be a masochist in love
to want someone so unattainable
that I would keep my life like a boomerang,
knowing each day that goes by
I am re-living the same moments repeatedly,
drowning in the depths of his oceans
with no signal for communication
or sign of life on land.

J. SAUNDERS

He was the Summer's Sun
I was the Winter's Moon

SECOND CHANCES

I continue screaming your name
as I reach out in search for you
after another nightmare.
Marco-Polo, takes two to play
still with eyes closed
arms out,
I call hoping you'll reply.

J. SAUNDERS

I'm tired.
My eyes are heavy.
Gut wrenching feeling in the pit of my stomach.
Hearts bleeding.
Holding myself.
I'm within myself
sitting in a black hole
nearly breathless,
loving you feels like the death of me.

NO MORE LOVE

You left me,
dealing with that was hard enough.

Put my heart back,
return my cigarettes and bottles of red wine.

I don't want to cry
empty and sober tonight.

J. SAUNDERS

LOVE AND LOVED

Honestly... I miss the nights with you beside me,
tucked beneath the covers
holding onto me too tight
as if I was going to sneak away.
Countless kisses behind my ear
while squeezing me in closer.
Those things and more
before the lies escaped between us.
Secrets whispered in the dark
unable to bring us back together.

SECOND CHANCES

I LEFT THE BIG PICTURE BEHIND

Life is constantly changing.
We were being forced to move on
with gravity, but we stood still.
Eventually something or someone must break
after years of constantly taking.

That something was us.
The someone was me.

I've broken down 100 times
since letting you go.

J. SAUNDERS

NO EXPLANATION

Loving you was deep.
I am still submerged.
So many parts of you
I wasn't able to reach,
I was too late.
You gave up on yourself,
you gave up on me.
Pulling me out from the bottom of your heart,
apologizing that this isn't a goodbye.
Soaking wet and broken
unsure where I went wrong
with no guarantee you'd be back.

SECOND CHANCES

It's been awhile and as of lately I find myself
searching for you within a crowd of people
hoping to get a glimpse of your smile,
disappointed when I go home with old memories.

J. SAUNDERS

I learned from the best
From the man who spilt my heart in two,
how to be cruel in the promise of love

SECOND CHANCES

You went from sweet texts and compromise,
to savagery and robbery,
wanting everything but giving nothing.

CYCLE CONTINUES

The air wreaked of last night's mistakes.
Ashes were all over the table,
cigarettes piled over,
empty wine glasses and left-over pizza,
neither of us leaving the entanglement
while the dawn crept between the blinds.

SECOND CHANCES

Loving you was my strength and weakness
Just like a pack of cigarettes I crave but never need

J. SAUNDERS

MADLY IN LOVE

Please don't come back
unless you're staying this time,
even If I say otherwise
don't listen to me.
We can never just be friends
and since I am no longer high on you,
you can't come back,
because I'm madly in love with you.
I can't play another round of lust
knowing it's my heart on the line.

SELF-REFLECTIONS

I don't want to be understood.
I don't need you to know every scar on my body.
What I need is to be loved.

You do not need to be a psychologist, philosopher or
scientist in order to love me.
It's not complicated.
You look at someone and unwillingly,
you want to give this person love and nothing else.

All I want is to be loved,
the rest we can figure out along the way.

J. SAUNDERS

I've been thinking about it.
I remember when I tried to leave,
you told me to wait.
You told me how good we were together
only to disappear and have me trip over you,
losing my mind over the conversations we had,
the memories we shared.
But eventually this confusion within will fade.
No longer will I beg for you;
instead I want someone to fight for me,
someone to hang off my every word,
look me in the eyes and never want to blink.
I want someone to
fight for my love and mean it.

SECOND CHANCES

I want the little things;
forehead kisses,
pancakes in bed,
a note on the mirror,
laughs that give you abs,
your arms as my embrace,
heart beating against my back,
to wake up and do it all again.

J. SAUNDERS

I can't stay here with you,
we weren't meant to be together
in this lifetime.
Maybe in the next one
we'll find each other first
before all the others,
and I understand
I've come to terms
knowing not everyone you love
will be in your life forever,
even if I don't agree.

SECOND CHANCES

OLD LOVE

It wasn't like I had a shitty week
or a rough month.
It was about 6 years of my life.
So, when people ask me why I never mentioned you
or talked about my past to explain who I am today,
I wouldn't know where to start.

It's then when people would know
I wasn't always this positive,
and treat me like I'm breakable.

LIAR

What better way to say you're sorry,
then to redo the same thing,
you apologized for?

SECOND CHANCES

THAT SECOND LOVE

When I got the news that you were engaged
it fucked me up a bit.

Not because I thought that would be us.
I just remember you tearing me apart
using my love to heal you.

For the same woman
you're about to promise
an eternity of love to,
after leaving my heart lifeless.

J. SAUNDERS

I was everything she wasn't.
To him this was great,
loving the opposite of what he was used too.
But his heart would never be mine,
it belonged to her.
We loved, only to let go.
She was his home.

SECOND CHANCES

REACTION

Eyelids with a permanent shade of pink.
Grey eyes desperately trying to be blue again.
Cracked lips from dehydration
tasting like last night's whiskey.

I'M TRYING

I'm sorry that I forgot how to love.
I know it's considered easy,
yet I found it difficult.

And I'm sorry you ran out of patience.
Proclaiming you once loved me,
stomping around and slamming doors.

Out of everything love has taught me
it's not fragile like we make it out to be.

SECOND CHANCES

MY LOVE

I am not the type of girl
who wants to fix or change you.

I've loved you just the way you are
since the first night I met you.

Also,
I'm not the type of girl who
manages very well.

Settling has never been my thing,
pick a side of the line between us.
Love or nothing,
uncertainty keeps me up at night.

BELLEZZA

Sometimes I close my eyes
reminiscing the way your
thumb would rub along the side of my ribs,
tracing the imprinted ink in admiration.

SECOND CHANCES

MOVING ON

Sitting on my bed
back against the wall;
lights off,
headset on,
unable to move,
listening to Adele,
reminding me
I cannot
love you in the dark.

J. SAUNDERS

You're always going to love me.
I'm that girl
that battled the war for your
love and you let me get away.

SECOND CHANCES

It's not always about
who you want
but who wants you too.

Who stays awake at night
wondering if they're on your mind
losing sleep like they are.

J. SAUNDERS

From afar they want me
lustful eyes and tempted fingertips.
They get close but never stay
after meeting me demons
then say, they are no match
for what's beyond my walls.

SECOND CHANCES

I've had trouble in the love department
since us,
since them.
The ones who thought they liked
or said, they loved me
never stayed – they didn't last.
I pushed them over the corners of my walls
because I had never healed and I'm short fused.
It's been a vicious circle within me,
I realize this now.
Willing to accept and relive the pain from my soul.
Let go of anything that has caused me detrimental pain
and move on with my life.
I can only control myself.
You, like the others
are my past.

Maybe... I didn't make myself clear.
I do not have room in my heart for cowards.

SECOND CHANCES

FIRST LOVE

I stopped feeling sorry for you. I stopped blaming myself for all the times you were depressed and unsure about life when I left. When for years you chipped away at my soul. Barely escaping. Leaving everything I loved behind because I felt I no longer needed to stay in ruins when I deserved sunsets.

So, I don't feel sorry for you.
Not even when you crawled back in desperation, with more lies. Begging on your knees for me but disgustingly unable to let go of her... just doesn't cut it for me.

You can go ahead and pick up the bricks from our past. You can build the biggest castle. Give me the brightest sun. The prettiest flowers to warm my heart.

I will never call you home again.

I do not feel sorry for your loss.

J. SAUNDERS

I don't write about the people who have hurt me
Comparatively, I write about the people I have loved

SECOND CHANCES

Someone is going to try and fill the shoes
you weren't man enough to fill.

Someone is going to try
and knock down the walls you turned away from.

Someone is going to battle the war for my heart,
that you were too much of a coward to do.

The women who remind you that a man will not make you whole, are the same ones, who felt their entire being shattered because they fell in love and now have nothing to show for it.

SECOND CHANCES

I often heard people say, that she was a beautiful woman, damaged but beautiful. She planted seeds in her wounds to watch flowers bloom, as she healed herself. All the wrong men will pick and pull, instead of offering water and sunlight.

Many men have gone her way and all of them have left with cuts from thorn bushes, after putting their hands in places they shouldn't be.

A beautiful woman, but damaged.

I was told that a rose is given as a symbol of love.
Buy her a dozen roses for valentine's day or even just
because. I've always viewed roses as a representation
of death. Families send roses to say, sorry for your loss
and you may circle a casket and place a single rose to say
goodbye. Either way, I've come to compromise.
When you fall in love, flowers like a rose should bloom. The
world seems like a better place to be in and the aroma is
fresh and sweet. Relish in it. Enjoy it. Every second. Every
sweet scent. Because when the love you once praised, if it
happens to wither away. As the rose petals begin to fall,
when the dying flowers create that horrible musk smell
because you failed to maintain them. You'll think of death.
Until you replace them and start again.

SECOND CHANCES

WHY I LEFT

You're absolutely right.
You did fuck up.
Everyone fucks up at least once or twice
but that's not why I left you.

I left because you were no longer
accountable and trustworthy.
You fucked up 100 times and then some.
Fucking up became a habit
between the sheets and hips of women who weren't me.
I looked like the other woman begging for attention,
questioning your anger when I would ask,
where you had been for hours.

Please don't tell yourself it's okay now
because I am strong enough to look you straight in the
face and smile,
like nothing ever happened.
Don't believe for a second
I'll ever look at you and think you're worthy for anyone.

You're unquestionably right,
they can have you.
I deserve anyone who isn't you.

J. SAUNDERS

With you I am everything.

Without you I am still everything.

I love everything I am, with you.

SECOND CHANCES

I am thankful for the days I never thought I'd make it.
For the moments when insanity had taken over.
When the butterfly photos on the wall covering holes from his fists were a part of illusions and they were flying free from my space.
When I slept alone for weeks after weeks in a cold room as if it was punishment.
Thankful for the days I carried strength
and the nights I broke down.
For the poetry book I once wrote titled Love Letters.
154 pages written like he wanted.
I knew love, but this was never love.
I am thankful for the time I fell to the floor;
back against the wall,
knees to chest,
mascara burning my eyes.
That night, the night I told you we were over,
your psychological and physical abuse stopped there.

All that's left to be done
is to pick up the broken pieces
and build a whole new woman.

Believe me
I loved you,
more than myself at one point.
I never needed you to love me back.
Unfortunately, in your
"effort" to love me instead of
her,
left me broken and in agony.

I'm brave enough to move on from you.

SECOND CHANCES

Do you ever get mad or are you always this understanding?
Do you not yell or have something terrible to say, or are you always this polite?

> When I met him, I vowed to do everything differently.
> I had spent so much of my last relationship
> screaming, fighting and crying,
> exhaustion had taken over.
> Truthfully, love drained
> me, and I just wanted to be loved for a
> change.
>
> I am not a jealous woman,
> I am kind and I love deep.
> I hate getting brutally angry;
> the screaming,
> throwing items across the room,
> being called crazy with no self-control,
> when all of this can be avoided
> with proper communication.
>
> I think the man who'll love me next
> will comprehend,
> that when I say,
> "I understand",
> there is a beast in hiding
> that just wants to be loved.

J. SAUNDERS

You didn't hurt me

I hurt myself.

You just stuck around

long enough to watch.

Long enough to say,

I told you so.

SECOND CHANCES

The beginning is always the hardest.
I remember wanting to mute the T.V commercials
because the new Mr. Clean segment
made a sound like your ringtone.

J. SAUNDERS

Things change
People change
Feelings change

        Things, people and feelings change,
              learn to let go

                      Overwhelmed in love
                        constant lies told

        Still I love the thought of you

Mr. Sun and sun kissed skin

      Every summer the Sun watches love stories unfold

                      Summer love affair

      Seasons change and so do the people

Learn to let go
it was the sun you loved
not the boy

SECOND CHANCES

I'm waiting for the pain to subside,
the love to fade,
to feel nothing at all
and start all over again.

LET GO

The words,
"you have to let him go",
echoed in the background of her soul.
While her heart clinched with pain,
screaming for mercy,
her eyes unable to stop the tears.
Somewhere beyond the noises
there was a quiet reply that said,
"I know",
as she wept harder.

SECOND CHANCES

If he wants you, if he loves you, he'll fight for you. There would be no other man for you. Believe me when I say, if someone so happened to have tried to take you and he doesn't rage a war like the Trojan War, when Helen was taken... he never loved you. Understand this.

J. SAUNDERS

Never be angry with yourself for falling in love

SECOND CHANCES

THE LAST PHONE CALL

You must forgive me
You have to forgive me, please
I hurt you, but I need you to forgive me
Will you ever forgive me?
Hello, love, please.

I beg of -

hard silence

J. SAUNDERS

The only person I need to forgive is myself

SECOND CHANCES

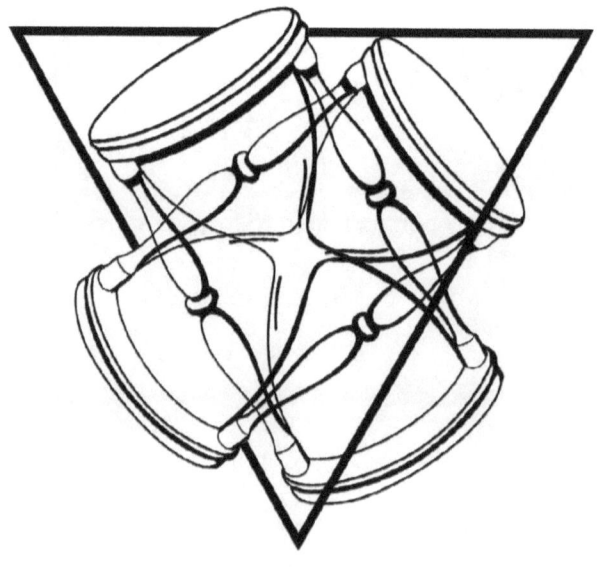

J. SAUNDERS

If there is one thing for certain
I will never lie to you.

To love... requires every fiber in you.
It's being able to love yourself
and someone else at the same time.

A breakup... requires every fiber in you,
to go through the emotional requirements
while carrying on with life as if your heart
doesn't feel like It's dying.

A friendship... requires every fiber in you,
the best friends become family
and require love like any other relationship.

Family... requires every fiber in you;
the give and take,
the fuss and love,
the pressure and worry.

You... being you requires every fiber in you.

If there is one thing for certain;
people are bat shit crazy,
people are emotional wrecks,
people are unbalanced,
people forget that happiness starts with themselves.
Not one single person is perfect
and if you tell me otherwise
I'd call you a liar.
that's okay 80% of people lie.
95% of people lie to themselves.

I was one of them
but I will not lie to you,
not this time.

SECOND CHANCES

Sometimes the voices get so loud
you're unable to tune them out.
They scream and echo
terrible things you don't deserve to hear.
It is unfair,
especially when you're having a good day.

Today the voices spoke to me. They
told me I wasn't good enough,
I wasn't loved, and no one would miss me.
I'll never amount to anything,
I should just go home and give up.

Sometimes the voices win.
The awful feeling in the pit of your stomach,
disappears with a pill or a nap.
You thought that would solve the problem,
because for a brief moment
time stood still and on your side.
When the haze wears off,
it's a hurricane of emotions
and self-doubt.

I am not in your shoes,
but I can tell you how to begin your battle.
Do the opposite of everything,
the demons try and make you do.

Remind yourself,
that you're not alone and you're worthy,
never let anyone or anything,
suggest differently.

Today I didn't go home,
I wrote this piece instead,
hoping it reaches someone in time.

BUTTERFLY EFFECT

Some people create storms
not realizing they created a hurricane else where.

SECOND CHANCES

You are beautiful.
You are your own kind of magic.
You are amazing in your own way.
Never let someone compare you
or take that away.

It's okay to cry about the emotions that are now upsetting
and killing your insides.
All at once, everything turned on you.
You weren't prepared to fall in love, nor will you be
prepared for the unwanted ugliness of pain.

SECOND CHANCES

I never needed saving
to be honest.
I never needed anyone
but it would be nice
to have someone
love me today
and not
turn on me tomorrow.

J.SAUNDERS

                                                I hope you still care
                                Even when they tell you not to
                              Even when they don't want you to

If you truly cared
wouldn't you always?

SECOND CHANCES

GO FOR IT

When the dust settles
you'll remember that life may not be effortless
or fair but you'll
go after what is meant for you.

When I thought my life was falling apart When I thought nothing around me could be saved, I found myself in the midst of it all

It was the best journey I could have gone on

SECOND CHANCES

One day
my memory will kill me,
until then
it creates the untold stories
that bring me back to life.

WHEN I FOUND LOVE AGAIN

He was technically
my second love
which is confusing
because his love
hit home more
than the first.

SECOND CHANCES

I met love again and thought I was no longer good enough.
Weakness from my battles lead me to let go of someone
who brought me nothing but joy.
I hope he's happy.

When you're so used to emptiness and pain.
Used to lies and abuse.
The truth from even the most trustworthy person
may never feel right,
learn to trust them anyways.
Not everyone has wrongful intentions.

SECOND CHANCES

You're feeling;
unsure, unloved, mistaken,
anxious, because you keep settling
for all the things your gut
is telling you to prevail through.

J. SAUNDERS

NEVER THE VICTIM

I am over being the nice one,
the one everyone walks on,
the quiet one
when I deserve to be heard.
I am over holding other people's blood
portrayed as my own.
I have been described as the victor
for far too long
by people who shouldn't be trusted
with a butter knife.

SECOND CHANCES

He didn't love me
He stayed anyways

You said, you loved me
before leaving like I was nothing

What makes you better than him?

J. SAUNDERS

I am not lost
I am simply on a path
that was only meant for me to understand

SECOND CHANCES

HER SIDE OF THE STORY

I became the woman I hated.
As time went on
I no longer cared about
the consequences life warns you about.
I began living and laughing.
Alone or with another
even if he wasn't mine,
he wasn't my man deceiving me.
I lost my way to lust and revenge.
Lost in the highs that eventually
became the lows.

It is my life to live but I owe someone an apology.

LOVE OR LET GO

I am not an old book for you to hold onto,
there is no value in a human
left alone and untouched on a shelf.

My binding won't last forever.

SECOND CHANCES

If he loved you,
I mean, truly loved you,
you wouldn't be alone
questioning everything
as if you,
did something wrong.

LIVE YOUR BEST LIFE

Everything takes time
and that's the problem,
you never know when you're
going to run out of it.

SECOND CHANCES

"You don't look like a poet.
You're too beautiful.", he said.
As if, beautiful people cannot be broken and damned.

J. SAUNDERS

You should be brave
wear your heart on your sleeve and love

Love, regardless of all the terrible things that have
happened and will happen
The world's a scary place I know

There will continue to be
evil things in the world
Wicked people will unfortunately lurk in the shadows

You need to be brave
remain true and kind
because if there is evil… there is good too

SECOND CHANCES

I know it's terrifying.

Take the leap of faith.

Fall in love with love.

Prince Charming isn't always the one who plays "the part". Rather the one who steals your heart, and plays music you'll always hear, but never know the source. He's captain hook, bad for you – your hearts in the bottom of the ocean, chasing the sunsets forever searching for love.

SECOND CHANCES

The same way a good man, deserves a good woman
    — a woman deserves a good man.

That is what we always forget.
It's about completing each other,
because our hearts are like empty tea pots until filled.

You're the tea bag, and
they're your water.

GIVE LOVE A TRY

What if what seems to be so great
shatters us into a billion pieces
and we're left alone?

What if what seems to be so great
fills us with love for a lifetime?

SECOND CHANCES

I cannot promise you
ever after or dry eyes

I can promise
the pain you're feeling
is temporary
He'll go away
and become a memory
You will laugh again

Take your time

J. SAUNDERS

CLEAN UP

Pardon my manners,
it's been awhile since I had anyone here.

Please, excuse the mess
I'm still cleaning fragments of the old me.

Throwing away pieces of an old love.

SECOND CHANCES

WHO I AM

I'm insane
Beautifully reckless unable to be tamed

There are four things I know
I cannot control:

the time,

my heart,

the weather,

our memories.

Forgive me, I am incapable of changing this even if I'm entitled to them.

SECOND CHANCES

I always expected the day I no longer loved you, there would be a celebration. Not literally but within myself. Assuming there would be this sensation relieved from my soul. Yet, time just kept going and I had nothing. I remember whenever I'd see 11:11 or I blew out a candle, I used to wish for you, for us. I used to pray for you, then us. I used to tell everyone they were wrong about you... about us. As time kept creeping by, I started looking back. Thinking on the days that have passed wondering if I missed the sign. I was hopelessly, trying to grab a hold of anything just to say, here you go. This is my token. My get out of jail free card. Nope, nothing and I would find nothing. By searching and spending my efforts trying
to relieve myself from you, I didn't realize the reason I never felt freedom, was because I held onto so much anger and resentment. There were so many emotions but never enough actions. So many memories, never enough words. Weak and fragile became me. I was hiding. I was running from the ghosts instead of facing them. Avoiding. I would avoid telling people my story, my life, the things I had been through because I was scared, I would be judged. Judged for loving and trusting you. For having a soul that wanted to reach out to others and save them, without realizing I was starving myself. I was starving my soul. From all the good places and good people... because I was searching for a lifeline. So, I'd go out in the world and would grab onto anything and anyone that didn't resemble you or what we were. I found love, and let it die in front of me because I didn't think it was worth it. I had no strength to pick up the sword and fight. Not just for him but for myself. Starving. I never found that token, and I never got that sensational feeling. What I got was myself instead.
I am my lifeline and I am no longer starving my soul on behalf of someone else. This includes you.

Love hurts.
There is nothing as painful as heartbreak
but in order to love again
you must first learn how to trust.

SECOND CHANCES

I want to love you in all the ways you've been neglected
take you to all the places you're scared to go alone to.

"You're not going to win the game of love that way" she said.
"I'm not playing" I replied.

SECOND CHANCES

UNDECIDED

I have known love at Its highest
It's sweet and full of devotion

I have known love at its lowest
It's painful and full of desperation

I am somewhere in the middle
holding onto anything I can find
Ignoring all the signs as if that's
not misery on its own

Standing in the middle
I still feel the sun
that must count for something right?

I am not lost.

                        Please do not come searching for me.

            I am hiding in all the places
                you cannot find me
                    on purpose.

EGGSHELLS

Since I am no longer
running around in circles.
No longer tiptoeing around,
hiding behind a woman
I thought the world wanted me to be.

I am at peace.

No one said,
you were wrong.

You're entitled to your opinions and feelings.

I'm just expressing mine.

SECOND CHANCES

Everyone is playing the same game.
Wanting someone to be there for them
without having the responsibility of returning
the favour and being there for them when needed,
because that would be called a relationship
and no one want's one of those these days.

The new dating pool.

J. SAUNDERS

The damaged ones know love the best
They wouldn't be broken if they didn't

EXCUSES

Hearing that I've been *keeping busy*
after weeks of not talking
is just another way of saying,
I found everything to do
but contact you.

It gets dark in here, did you know?
When the light runs out
and you're in pitch black darkness.

Gets chilly in here too, did you know?
Since there's no other source of heat
because it was your warmth that kept me warm.

Also, it gets quiet in here sometimes, did you know?
When the echoes finally stop from my screams, you could
hear a pin drop.

You did this, did you know?

You brought me to the center of my heart
asked for my love,
and drained me;
turning black,
developing cracks,
leaving only one thing
left within my empty heart,
me.

SECOND CHANCES

I'll stop caring
Eventually
Though that seems far away
It resembles your distance

That's what I tell myself

How about
you, and every other man child
who doesn't know what he wants
stays the hell away
from women,
who know, what they want.

SECOND CHANCES

A woman's intuitions is stronger, and will last longer than a man's dick prepared to fuck.

J. SAUNDERS

From time to time
I wish there was a man to hold,
to trust,
to love,
because I know loneliness.
I am just a woman
who is scared to fill this void
after countless men since
have failed to provide me love,
once seeing my body with lecherous eyes.

SECOND CHANCES

LIFE IS WORTH THE LAUGH

It doesn't matter how old you are today.
Life never gets easier.
There will always be a bump in the road
and I'd like to think,
that although nothing is certain
I hope the bumps in my life say,
you laugh too loud.

J. SAUNDERS

> I pray
> you stop attaching yourself
> to all the wrong people.

SECOND CHANCES

Very few people
will click with you.
It's like their soul
connects with yours
nearly instantly.
It's those types of people
who you fight for
and love unconditionally.

BE HONEST

What is the point in fighting the truth?

It only leads way for reality
to be that much harder to face
when the lies surface from their hiding place.

SECOND CHANCES

Yes, I know
the right one will come along
and take away all the pain of yesterday.
That's what they say,
and women sit around praying someone heals them
instead of standing up and healing themselves.

J. SAUNDERS

If only they knew the woman they admired for her strength, would cry in her car if she couldn't make it home in time.

SECOND CHANCES

I love
    touching
    kissing
    holding
        you

                I love,
              loving you
        from your darkest corners
        to your beautiful smile.

J. SAUNDERS

BE CAREFUL

He doesn't deserve to
occupy that much of your mind
while running in and out
of your life,
as if there is a door
with his name on it.

SECOND CHANCES

If you're looking for a temporary fix to your lonely nights
I am the wrong girl for you. I leave impressions that last
longer than an hour between the sheets.

I know my worth
and it's not a one-night stand with you.

J. SAUNDERS

By the time they realize your worth
I hope you weren't waiting around.
> *- Time wasted*

SECOND CHANCES

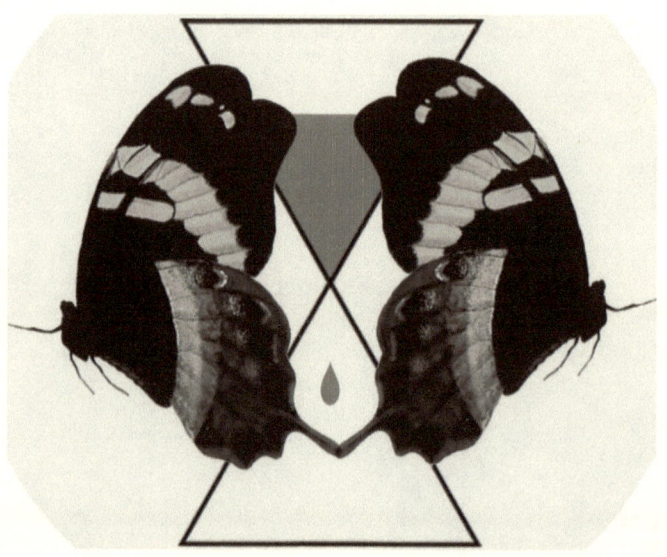

J. SAUNDERS

We can stand in the sun
for as long as we want,
but if you don't know
when to put the umbrella away
and dance in the rain
it'll never work out between us.

SECOND CHANCES

All women usually ask for is an apology from their ex
and to be honest I've never understood why.
It's like the need for closure after telling him to leave you alone.
Why hurt yourself just to hear the man who hurt you say,
some pathetic apology when he obviously
didn't care enough about you in the first place.
It's horrible I know,
but I'd rather another man apologize saying,
he's sorry for not finding me first and holding me with love
than another lie from the one who hurt me.

Every woman knows their worth
until they fall in love
and somehow forgets who they are.

Don't let that be you.

You can fall in love
and still be Wonder Woman.

Anyone who tells you differently
falls into the hands of people
who don't want them to know their potential.

SECOND CHANCES

She's everything you're looking for in a woman.
She's independent, an alpha.
She has a tough exterior with a soft heart.
She is kind, loving, sexual and selfless.
She knows how to treat a man
and when God, gives her the right one
she'll give her heart away, unconditional love.

J. SAUNDERS

Eventually, the pain will fade
and your era of self-pity will wear off.

You will ignite the flames
that were once ashes within you,
burning stronger and higher
than the woman they used to reside in.

SECOND CHANCES

You left
I nearly didn't survive.
Countless thoughts
saying, "you're going to die...
who are you, without him?".

For a moment in time
this was my life
but like a Phoenix
I rose from the ashes.

I am everything without you.

I LOVED THE BIGGER PICTURE

I miss you at times and places least expected.
In those moments I feel the empty spaces that were once
loved. Missing you has become a norm in my daily routine.
I am no longer sad or filled with regret.
My heart no longer begs for you when the sun goes down.

I just miss you.
Simple as that.

SECOND CHANCES

STOP

Putting your hopes,
your goals,
your dreams,
into someone else.

Take all that shit
and put it solely into yourself.

You are what makes
all that good shit possible,
not them.

My entire life all I've heard is, to stay pretty and remain strong. As if women like me weren't supposed to read books and conquer mountains.

SECOND CHANCES

I destroy myself because I give away my love better than 7/11 gives out free slushies' in the summer, knowing people are going to abuse the rules and rip me off, of my one time offer.

You are a storm
Carrying all the energy you'll ever need within you

SECOND CHANCES

I believed in you
You were a liar
It hurt
Life goes on

But doesn't it?
Isn't that the first step to taking the band-aid off?
Acknowledging and accepting the truth?

Even if it hurts

J. SAUNDERS

NEW BEGINNINGS

Isn't that the way it always goes with you?
You never let anyone in
and when you do,
it's one wall closer.

You have like 20,
why don't you break a few down?
You act as if all men are the same.

You want love but
refuse to give up what hurt you.

So, either I'm just not the one,
or you love me
and won't give up your previous losses.

You cannot have it your way all the time.
I'm not afraid to look you straight in the eyes,
and tell you, with conviction that
I love you.

But I will not always be brave.
I need you to meet me halfway;
at least tell me
when I say,
I love you, you at least believe me,
that you feel me not just hear me.
Tell me I am fighting for something,
when you ask me to stay
after wiping tears off your face.

May I come in,
after all this time?

SECOND CHANCES

How much longer
of this game
shall we play?
When we're
both on our knee's
begging for love
to take us.

J. SAUNDERS

Suddenly, I didn't understand anymore.
Life seemed so unfair,
and I decided,
I would take back what is mine.
Like my heart, for starters.

SECOND CHANCES

I'm just trying to
hold it all together
Since meeting you
I stumble at times
after falling in love

Would've, could've, should've.

The three things,
I'm absolutely, not interested in discussing.

SECOND CHANCES

Stop holding onto
all the people &
things
that you used to know.

This includes yourself.

J. SAUNDERS

Letting go of someone you love,
is life's way of reminding you,
never to build your home in someone else.

Someone please tell me,
how do I know, who to give myself to?
My love is not a coin toss,
but we throw ourselves at people,
hoping they throw themselves back at us.

SECOND CHANCES

I'm not going to be the one
who tells you to let go and move on.
Breaking up with someone you love
is losing more than someone beside you at night.
You're no longer having this person in your life,
take a moment to grieve.
Take as long, as your heart needs,
just never sit at rock bottom blaming yourself.
Accept your loss and transition into life.
Naturally things begin to be normal again.

LOVE AGAIN

Just because someone broke your heart doesn't mean
you're not capable of love again.
Love never leaves your soul.
There is no limited amount or expiry on it.

SECOND CHANCES

In case I never get to let you know
face to face,
there are no more skeletons in my closet collecting dust.
My demons are free,
I am no longer tormented by the ghosts of you.

J. SAUNDERS

Many men may proclaim to admire
one's beauty and intelligence.
However, are unable to hold a conversation longer than an
hour without making a sexual comment as if their ego isn't
pouring out of their pores.

BE HONEST

Look at me
tell me you don't want me in your life.

Tell me you don't need me
so I can be on my way.

You are worthy.
You are worthy of happiness.
You are worthy of love.
You are worthy of the dreams you desire.
You are worthy of healthy relationships.
You are worthy
                of anything
    you want or need
without question.

SECOND CHANCES

In the blink of a moment.
Second to a minute,
that's how fast your life can change.

I will still love you when you're not here.

How nice is it to know
when you're awake and alone in the middle of the night
knowing someone out there
loves you?

- I'll be your someone

SECOND CHANCES

If you want to win the game of love
you first must love yourself
and tell those who matter,
then those who cross your path
that you are worthy of only pure,
honest love,
nothing more.
Nothing less.

Accepting anything other than what you want, is settling.
You have no idea what the magic of tomorrow can bring.

If the past was meant to shape me,
determine who I am today,
you would not be reading this.
Between the people and places of physical and mental destruction, strength is not determined by your current abilities, but the living proof that when everything was wrong you had the strength to prevail and change the outcome.

SECOND CHANCES

I have been fighting people and life for far too long.

If you do not bring me peace
you must leave.

My love is no longer a battle field.

J. SAUNDERS

People come and go,
this, I understand.
Although, I wish you had stayed,
circumstances changed, I understand.
How you leave my life,
determines if you can return.
There are no emotions,
only facts of past judgment.
Do you understand?

SECOND CHANCES

You never move on because you want to. You move on because you have to. At first, it's shitty. Your heart feels like it's at the bottom of your stomach. You're nervous and you can't get them off your mind. Eventually it'll all fade. The gut wrenching feeling will go away. You'll realize you're safe without them. Although you'll maybe wish about the would've and could've, you'll have enough strength to know, you're no option. You're not a debate. You're a yes or no. No one deserves uncertainty and lengthy break ups.

J. SAUNDERS

Do not be afraid
if you've wandered off course lately
Life is not one straight line
nor with the same faces of people you know
and never with the same emotions
Do not stop yourself from the experience,
the rollercoaster life is trying to give you

SECOND CHANCES

I can't tell if I am lost or being found.
The person inside, she is scared... a nervous wreck.
Anxiety eats me alive at times.

J. SAUNDERS

Perhaps, you should love yourself more,
not for someone else to see or to understand
but because in the end...
what better way to know love,
than from within?

SECOND CHANCES

YOU GOT THIS

Sometimes the demons win by default
I understand
The same way I look in the mirror
and I'm unable to recognize the woman that I see
but still I tell her,
don't you dare give up
You want to sulk about it
then sulk and when you're done,
you get the hell up and you try again

    - I am you
      You are the woman in the mirror

Standing in the center of my shower shaking,
unable to stand up straight any longer.
Trying to grip a slippery bathroom wall
I forced myself to turn off the water.
Forced myself to get out.
I felt like every fiber in me was going to fall to the ground.
Soaking wet I stumbled to my bed,
sitting on the edge of it while my legs convulsively shake.
This was it.
This was me realizing that you were not going to be there
to help me.
This was me realizing I'm on my own.
This was a moment of my wounds opening after I swore, I
healed them. I had to let go and I had to move on. Violently
shaking I'm going to faint.
My hands are shaking,
knee caps buckling.
My gut is killing - it's hurting.
I'm uncontrollably crying,
I'm going to move on.
This is a panic attack.
This is going to pass and I am no longer going to feel this
way towards you, nor self-conflict this against myself.
Maybe not today or tomorrow,
but eventually,
I am no longer going to feel the sense of urge for you.
I will no longer want to revisit my places of pain,
I will move on from this moment.
This is a panic attack.
It came out of nowhere and I am unable to stop it.
Its uncontrollable.
I was just taking a shower...
but it will be okay,
I will be okay.

SECOND CHANCES

There is no turn off button.
There is no correct medication a doctor can give.
Years can pass, and anorexia may haunt me.
Anxiety disorder can still take over.
Depression still knocks on my door.
The brain is a powerful organ,
constantly it needs flourishing,
reinforcements of love to maintain
a healthy relationship with your heart and soul.

J. SAUNDERS

You cannot fix someone
only love them,
and hope it reaches them in time.

SECOND CHANCES

Beyond the talking voices
I hear the clock to my right
ticking violently loud.

I am alone at work
and alone at home.

All I have is myself
and the talking voices.

Slowly, I am beginning to understand
why things seem insane,
things meaning me.
Why I am tripping over myself,
having conversations with the voices.
The clock has nothing useful to add
except to tell me when to change locations.

J. SAUNDERS

I allowed sorrow to take over.
In complete agony I held my body tight
pain from all negative,
horrible things people had done to me,
were doing to me.
All the self-pity,
I cried for the love in my heart, I
keep refilling to give to others
instead of myself.
Succumbing my thoughts to silence
feeling every emotion,
I'll never be the same because of it.
I felt my soul cry that night,
you can't come back from that.

SECOND CHANCES

I'm exhausted from
only knowing one side of love.
It hits hard and hurts deep.

J. SAUNDERS

What did you expect me to do?
Fall out of love with you with the snap of my fingers
all because you walked out the door?

My love has never and will never work that way.

SECOND CHANCES

I will not lie
I am a mess.

A beautiful mess, he replied.

Although his remark made me smile.

I've been lost.
Battling my scales
of loving too much
or loathing too hard,
I am no longer the
woman he once knew.

The more I confessed my inner voice
I couldn't help but feel further apart from myself.

Me: "So, why did it end if she made
you happy, if you loved her?"

Her: "... I fell in love with her laugh
and never told her."

It was the saddest ending
to a love story
I had ever heard.

DAY TO DAY

Today was a good day
and just when I thought the tears ran dry
my eyes swelled up
as I laid down to rest
Distracting my mind only works
for so long until my heart
asks to be felt,
releasing myself from drowning within

Feels like the ocean has dragged me to the bottom of its entity, and although I see the sunlight and I can make an approximate idea of how far I am from the surface. I do not think of the how and why, instead I'm focusing on the sharks and the killer whales. I just wanted to see a starfish. I just wanted to swim with the dolphins and somehow, I ended up here. The bottom of the ocean, so close to hell I can feel it's warmth. Bring me home or let me go.

SECOND CHANCES

It is true, I am a savage with my words
because my hands are weapons
and I lack control when pushed over the edge.

J. SAUNDERS

MY SECOND CHANCE

I postponed this for so long because I think that was all I had left. My words. My memories and the things no one knew. Maybe I wasn't ready to let go, I'll never truly know. I can only express what I knew and how scared I was to move past the gated fences of the unknown. It also meant I had to give up and let go of the past I once worked so hard to build. I was shattered on the floor. I didn't know how to pick myself up either.

Most days I just left myself there. I didn't bother to try and make effort to put myself back together. I went on with life, broken and confused. I stood by and allowed someone else dictate to me what my future should be, as if there were never any other options. This was it. The miserable place you call home with a man who doesn't love you and you love too much.

Try telling yourself that every day before you consider jumping out the window. I avoided my own truth in fear of myself. Pointing fingers at others who had well moved on with their lives, as I left myself behind. Once I was ready. Once I understood the common concepts of self-love and not relying on other people to make myself happy. When I understood my cries for escape were useless when I had become free and owed no one validation except for myself. I left my missing and damaged pieces on the floor for years. I found other ways to heal myself. To get through the day and make tomorrow, "the day" I face my fears. I managed to. Managed to pick up the pieces of my old self and truthfully, I tossed most of her in the trash. Everything she was, is everything I am not.

The remaining pieces are the scars of my history to remind me of who I was, where I came from, and everything I am not. It's never too late to start again, this is how I started.

SECOND CHANCES

Reach for me when in sadness
I may not be able to fix the broken parts,
but I can mend the pain.
Forgive me I am not perfect.
Pull me down under
I'll be your company
until the nightmare is over.

Your happiness is worth everything to me.

J. SAUNDERS

I love myself enough
to love you and I both
when you are in need
of self-love.

SECOND CHANCES

I learned that love will not always be a two-way street
and I hope you learn to embrace that
but never waste it.

The problem was you,
making me feel guilty for loving you.

The problem is,
I allowed myself to
believe in your bullshit.

Not everything or everyone comes with a
price or reason,
with intentions on ruining you.

SECOND CHANCES

Don't you ever get tired
from being everyone else
but yourself?

Please

    Be

        Kind

            To

                Yourself

SECOND CHANCES

The woman I am today,
you wouldn't know her. I
have evolved,
way beyond you
and the past.

Hey, remember when you called me a liar, a whore, an attention seeker when I told you what that man did to me? Remember when you told me you were disgusted by me, unable to look at me, unable to have me touch you? Remember when you screamed at me and slammed your hand on the counter while I made you dinner, laughing and mocking the day's I longed to forget. I just wanted to let you know, that I do not hate you anymore. Let you know, that I understand you were just a child and not the one for me. That someone was meant to love me, and that person just wasn't you.

SECOND CHANCES

I looked within myself only to learn how much of a mess I was. Where do I begin after neglecting myself for so long?

The hardest part in my life wasn't letting go of all the terrible things you had done to me. But moving on from what was, to what should be. The ruins that were left behind, I rebuilt. Working effortlessly not just on my home, or my mind, but my heart. My soul. I became bitter and so desperately wanted revenge. Focusing all my energy on rebuilding every aspect of my life as a means to say, fuck you. I never needed you. This is true, in reality, I needed myself more. My energy and time was going in all of the wrong places. It had taken me four years to evolve, I have become softer inside, but also stronger in all the right ways, happier and kind. I am now able to say, I love myself, when love from another was once unkind. Rebuilding a life, is a continuous effort, do not stop yourself from building yourself. I am still evolving, please keep evolving. Lastly, be gentle with yourself, life is hard enough on its own. Reread that and smile at the growth you have achieved if another human once tried to change that.

SECOND CHANCES

I am not afraid to start over.
I've come to understand that once you lose everything
you thought was your world,
you learn how to move on and
live with everything else instead.
All the things you were meant to have.

J. SAUNDERS

Law of attraction
is not something you beg for,
it is what you declare.
What you want and work hard for
while unfolding the opportunities to receive it.

SECOND CHANCES

I used to say,
my future is anything worth waiting for,
because it's everything with you.
Now it's unwritten with no plans,
turning into whatever I want it to be,
for me.

J. SAUNDERS

YOU'RE NOT ALONE

I will be there
even when you think
I am not.
On the days you're unsure,
never be afraid to ask.

It's okay that you have moments,
no one is perfect.
Those conflicting thoughts
I know about them,
still I love you,
I will continue to love you.

Your mind and your heart
are two different entities,
it is your heart I love.
The rest is magic in between.

SECOND CHANCES

I remember when I used to avoid the train.

There was this feeling to fall off the edge.
That bold yellow line I'd stand on
instead of behind,
seeing bright lights drawing me in
until I felt the pressured air
rushing into me forcing me to step back.

Sitting in my car today
looking at the clock
wondering if it's too late
to pay a visit to the train station.

This was real life for me.
A real thought and it puts people into perspective when the truth comes out. Depression is sometimes so silent, hidden behind big eyes and beautiful smiles, you wouldn't know if someone is hurting. Please, be kind.

J. SAUNDERS

STAY POSITIVE

Darkness is found even on the brightest days.
How you react to the shadows casted
says a lot about who you are.

SECOND CHANCES

I always wondered if an abuser preplanned their attacks or does something instantly take over and they must respond. I ask, what are their intentions, what gets them off by having someone who doesn't want them?
What are they searching for? Anything?
I know people have used drugs and alcohol as an excuse because being under the influence of any substance makes assault of any kind, somehow different than someone sober. I'm just wondering... why and I don't think I'll ever get the answer I'm searching for. Why anyone would ever want to commit such a crime to another human being, I believe is far beyond my capabilities in understanding. No medical thread could change my mind on the cases of people who are sexually assaulted and can't come back from it. What is an attackers punishment if never caught? Why must a victor win over a victim?

These are my wavering thoughts.

J. SAUNDERS

SOMEONE LOVES YOU

Whatever time it happens to be when you read this page,
morning, afternoon or night,
I want you to know that there
is someone who loves you.
There is quietly someone
in the background constantly supporting you.
They're routing for you to be happy and successful,
whatever those two words mean to you.

I dare you to smile.
I dare you to channel your inner you, and tell yourself
that you're proud of everything you are today.
Any challenges or no challenges at all,
whatever you could be going through,
you're going to make it past the dark sides of the sun.
Life is rough and society is fucked.
You are doing your best and that's all that matters.

I dare you to let go of the fear you currently feel.
If you feel caged
set yourself free.
You're magic, there is only one you,
on that sheer fact alone
you should own that.

Celebrate you.
Most importantly, love yourself
and remember
life is a rollercoaster
but someone loves you.

SECOND CHANCES

Other people will not heal you.
The love you are searching for
will not fix your broken parts,
if you are not looking within yourself.
Self-love is your cure.

It'll never be easy. Life.

It's never perfect and something you must take at face value. I can only suggest you grab onto it like a bull and take it for a ride. Laugh and enjoy the ups and downs it'll bring. The Lord, gives the toughest battles to those who can carry the strength to face it. Maybe you're not religious. That's okay. So, I'll tell you this. When your moments seem too heavy to bare I want you to think of the ocean. Even for all its beauty and strength the dependency is constant. At some points, she's shallow and breathtaking. Looking at her surface can be mesmerizing. She can also swallow you whole and show you the bottom of her many die to discover. Calm and peaceful moments can transpire into brutal and damaging events. You're like the ocean. Full of depth, full of hope and beauty. So many imperfect flaws yet in so many ways, flawless. Let the morning rays of new beginnings show you. It'll never be easy, life. It'll just be worth living for tomorrow.

WHAT WOULD LIFE BE LIKE?

Have you ever wondered or pictured what life would be like
without all the betrayal and pain that tainted you
over a duration of time?
Think about it, what if you let it all go?
What if you start to live your life the way you imagine it
instead of focusing on all the things that went wrong?

What would life be like?
The way it should be.

J. SAUNDERS

I dare you to be yourself

                and

                                say what you mean

SECOND CHANCES

I've only known of Whiskey
and a blank page
desperately waiting to be
filled with ink.

J. SAUNDERS

You must stop
proving yourself to people.

Especially to those who
don't trust themselves.

It's not easy to work on yourself
while justifying your actions to someone else.

SECOND CHANCES

All everyone wants
is for someone to
love and accept them
for everything they are
on the surface,
down to the unknown corners
To be loved with,
the 100 different masks
they wear for society,
and their heart
Then all their
madness in between

J. SAUNDERS

If you want to stay
you must know
that my love
is not temporary
and if you decide to leave
understand that my heart
remains with me.

SECOND CHANCES

If they, meaning male or female
wanted you,
they'd have you.

Too many of us walk around
with false hope
and unfulfilled promises.

Stop falling in love with people who don't want you.

Who use, lie, and drain all your energy.

Fall in love with someone who understands your madness and is there to stay.

SECOND CHANCES

LESSON LEARNED

I too am human
I make mistakes
and learn from my pain

J. SAUNDERS

Us humans are so much like the seasons, mother nature provides our growth and changes over a duration of time, phasing us into who we're supposed to be.

SECOND CHANCES

"... and if you don't do what I say..."

As I feel the muzzle of a hand gun
placed against the back of my head.

Needless to say,
I wasn't scared of the gun,
rather the person holding it
asking God, who was in control.

J. SAUNDERS

Each time you hurt or shatter,
pick up your broken pieces
and put yourself back differently.

Learn from the men,
who turned out to be boys.
The women, who
were small minded and petty.
The family, you've loved and lost.

You grow when you realize,
people and situations
are temporary;
it's always quality over quantity
and becoming so in tune with yourself,
that eventually,
you become unbreakable.

FEARFUL

I was more concerned with what he was going to think, feel and say.

Rather than what I felt, thought and wanted.

J. SAUNDERS

Take your time with me
or find someone else to waste it with.

SECOND CHANCES

THROW IN THE TOWEL

You don't get to just give up and throw in the towel.
Who the hell taught you to be lesser than what your capabilities are worth? If you're unable to come up with a solid answer to that question, I suggest you tell yourself, that you got this while telling society to go fuck itself. You don't get to give up, not today, tomorrow or the next day.

Not the following day either.
Pick up your towel and fight for yourself;
your goals,
your dreams,
whatever fuels you to wake up.
That passionate tingling feeling
you get when doing something you love,
do more of it.

Pick up the damn towel and live your life. It's yours after all.

J. SAUNDERS

FLY GIRL, FLY

A woman doesn't suddenly grow wings,
she learns how to spread them,
then soars.

SECOND CHANCES

She is better than your morning coffee.
Stronger than your glass of cognac.
She's the woman you'll say, is too much for you,
then look back and wish you never let her go.

Please, stop trying to find yourself in other people.

SECOND CHANCES

He didn't treat you right
you know this,
I know this.
You know that,
there is better out there
but that's not what
you're looking for right now.

You're looking for comfort
in someone else's words
to say, that they know
what you're going though
and the truth is,
I'm not in your shoes.

I'm not going to tell you,
that you're suddenly going
to wake up and
the pain is going to go away.
I will say,
that eventually,
it's going to be okay
and that's what matters.

We all shatter,
we're all breakable,
it's not how we fall apart that matters
but rather
how we put ourselves back together.

SECOND CHANCES

If he wanted to call,
believe me he would.

Once you allow excuses,
you find they never run dry.

If he wanted to see you,
he'd be at your door.

Stop settling for the vicious cycle,
you deserve better.

J. SAUNDERS

CONTRADICTIONS

Walls are caving in.
Heartbeat irregular.
Everything is spinning.
Tightness in my chest.
To think I can gain control
of something so uncontrollable.
I suffer within my body,
begging to escape yet love
myself at the same time.

SECOND CHANCES

One day a man will love you
instead of looking at you as a sexual dessert.

J. SAUNDERS

DON'T GIVE UP

The past will never go away,
one day you won't regret your previous choices.
You'll decide what day that is and when you do
your past will no longer haunt you.

SECOND CHANCES

There is nothing wrong with wanting to believe in the magic of true love.
The outcome may not be exactly what you're expecting.
The timing may not be what you dreamed of.
As long as you stay true; honest and bold, what was meant to be for you, will just be.

4:25AM

Restless and unable to sleep
I turn to my pen and paper
desperately hoping
this is the last piece
and my heart will let me rest.

FOR THE THIRD TIME

I am not lost.

Simply unexplained emotions,
unmentioned thoughts,
written down and unread.

It'll never be easy
but the feeling
will be worth it.

True love is first known from within

PRE-MEDITATED MURDER

I will remain single until proven it's safe to give away my love again. Too many people throw themselves at the first person who smiles. Lonely nights can cause blindness from desperation, thus, picking the devils pawns rather than God's chosen one.

Truth is, I have no idea what I am doing.
Daily I fail at something.
By realizing and admitting this,
I am ready to accept what is meant to be.
Now able to take on tomorrow without
repeating the same mistakes.

Remember to grow yourself daily

SECOND CHANCES

Should you ever feel unworthy from a man,
pack your things and leave.
Tell yourself you are beautiful and worth it.
Take a moment and focus all your energy on yourself.
You do not need someone like him.
You are not his property nor his trophy.
Be the woman you are and live the life you deserve.

J. SAUNDERS

You will never be
that someone to me.
You are someone to me.
My heart will always know the difference,
if you ever need a reminder.

SECOND CHANCES

Writing has gotten me through love and pain,
anxiety attacks and severe depression.
Writing is more than a passion,
it's every fiber of my body
written in words.

J. SAUNDERS

Losing you broke my heart,
then taught me how badly
I needed to love myself.

SECOND CHANCES

In my mind I am so much more.
Life is nothing like what it seems.
I am a visionary woman
who is determined to live out her dreams.

OLD FRIEND OF MINE

You're the type of person
who is so desperate for love and attention,
that you'll ruin anything in your path just to get
that temporary satisfaction.

Then when that person is done using you as a distraction
stops texting and calling you on a regular basis, you begin
walking back, hoping to pick up the pieces of everything
you let fall apart.

You can do this once,
maybe twice,
but once it's clear that this is a routine, many will
slowly pick up the pieces themselves
and walk in a different direction.

I'll miss you
but I picked up my pieces.

SECOND CHANCES

Remember when you said,
my battle,
was our battle. I
wasn't alone,
you too
were in this,
together we prevailed.

Which is why I wonder
why can't
your battle,
be our battle,
what's so different?
You're not alone.
I'm here on the side lines
dying to fight for you.

J. SAUNDERS

Lean on me
I won't tell
Even the strongest
Need somebody

SECOND CHANCES

Let me be a woman.
Let me, be me.

Life is a mess. Chances are you're going to fall
People are unkind, but you should be kind always.
Strength isn't just an appearance
but the person you become after the battles.

SECOND CHANCES

I was told that happiness was a rare thing to find, so I looked within myself.

J. SAUNDERS

LOVE YOURSELF!

I choose love each and every time
for love wins any battle of hate.
Let the enemies roar,
silence speaks louder.

I choose failure over success,
for there are more lessons in failing
than waking up with a silver spoon.

I picked me
because I may have been born alone
but I was loved before I was met,
then loved throughout my years
of defeat and heart breaks.

If my mother could still love me
I owe her more than life,
least I could do was love me too.

SECOND CHANCES

HOW DO YOU DO IT?

People ask me all the time, "how do you do it?".

I do it by understanding that I constantly fail.
I am not perfect, so I am bound to make mistakes.
By realizing this, it means there is less of a chance
I'll make the same mistake twice.
I am then ready and prepared to
have a better tomorrow. You get stronger daily.

There is never a day that goes by
where I don't question myself,
or have a moment of self-doubt,
or literally ponder,
how am I going to do it?
In that same moment,
I know, I am unstoppable.
It doesn't matter what I've been through,
who's around me
or what people think.

I believe it comes down to figuring out
how do you want to see yourself?
When you look at yourself and think back to the day you had,
I hope you'd want to feel proud of yourself,
have the encouragement to wake up tomorrow
and do it all again – live.

I still crumble and face anxiety issues,
I may have a break down and not move for an hour.
Understanding that this is happening,
I focus on how to move forward
and spend the remaining 23 hours of my day rather
than the one hour I lost.

I am not a selfish person by any means,
being a "savage" isn't my forte.
In that same sentence I deserve
anything and everything I want.
To achieve that, I must work hard.
Beat the odds and prevail in the things I love.

Take back what's mine.

What is it that you want?
You can achieve the impossible.

BE AUTHENTIC

If you continue to keep pretending,
lying and envying others,
eventually your fake life
will unfold with aggression you never thought
the Lord, could show you in such a lesson.

J. SAUNDERS

I aspire to be more daily.
Mentally, emotionally and physically.
Every day I do things that allow me to grow,
grow into being a better me.
People keep asking what I am doing in my life
and the truth is,
I am doing anything
that makes me happy.

SECOND CHANCES

I KNOW BETTER

I cared about him before myself
It was my biggest mistake
Even if love was worth it
I'm always worth more

J. SAUNDERS

At some point in your life,
you're going to change.

It's not a matter of why or how,
but when,
that is important.

SECOND CHANCES

I want you every night
even the nights
you don't want yourself.

- I love you the way you are

Just remember,
there is always tomorrow.

SECOND CHANCES

Sometimes you just run out of words
and all you're left with are the emotions
that were attached to them.

Beware of the people who say that they have commitment issues. They're the same people who have committed to nearly a lifetime of friendships.

SECOND CHANCES

Give me adventure.
A cliff to jump off.
A mountain to climb.

Give me passion and excitement,
wild and free.
Unexpected but unconditional,
anything but average.

This is how I want my love to be.

J. SAUNDERS

WHO'S RESPONSIBLE

It's not me
It's you
Still I faulter

SECOND CHANCES

You don't see
what I see

I understand
as I become blind
by your beauty

J. SAUNDERS

Sorry, if I came off too strong
Sometimes I care about people

But someone like me needs to apologize
Society is either too sensitive or unable to know kindness

SECOND CHANCES

There's a moment in each day
where the silence is a message
being delivered to you.
Open your heart
and listen to the universe
speak to you.

ANXIETY KILLER

Continue lurking in my shadows,
haunting me.
For each moment
you spend thinking I am weak.
I am preparing for victory,
when I demolish you.

Just because she smiles and keeps her emotions under control doesn't mean she hasn't been through a disaster.

HE ASKED

What do you want from me?

Nothing.
I want nothing from you.
I want to relieve the heaviness from your chest and love you.

SECOND CHANCES

Tell me where it hurts.
Your goals and dreams.
Tell me what you're needing and missing,
we'll start there.

J. SAUNDERS

UNSENT LETTER

It couldn't have been love,
still I believed in us
when the lust faded
and left me unguarded.
All I have are the quiet voices
repeating all the words
you once said to me.

SECOND CHANCES

I don't think you ever fall out of love with someone.
However, the first step to healing is acknowledging yourself.
Accepting the person you used to be,
and the person you'll become
once you move on from them.

J. SAUNDERS

DO YOU EVEN KNOW HOW TO LOVE?

The ones who seem impossible to break
are the ones who love the deepest.

SECOND CHANCES

Sometimes you're just over being alone.
I understand that loneliness can creep in.
Just hold onto yourself and the power of time just a little bit longer. Don't give up your worth by leaning into the arms of any person to keep you company. It can destroy everything you've become with the haze of desperation from wanting another person's hands on you.

Calling you months later with the words
I miss you;
I'm sorry,
doesn't mean he means it
and since realizing how good you were,
doesn't mean you crawl back.
They call you to try and bring you home.
Have a backbone.

You are your home

SECOND CHANCES

Never did I want
what everyone else did
nothing has made me want
a Disney type of love.

But rather a love like
how the Moon,
loves the Sun.

Not everyone will understand that.

Everyone is fighting some kind of battle.
Smile and bright eyes isn't the definition of happiness.
Sadness isn't a tear on a face, but words unsaid from the heart.
Be kind.
You can change someone's life with a simple hello.

SECOND CHANCES

You are not perfect
still I am proud of you.

The person you are today,
the person you will grow into
and all your imperfections.

J. SAUNDERS

NOTHING LEFT FOR ME

I was half alive for so long,
I forgot how to love.
I was breaking until you came around.
Everyone was always taking.
You breathed life into my lungs.
You resuscitated my heart,
steady beat, growing glow.
You were a sin dressed as an angel,
still I took your hand,
and left the woman I knew behind.

SECOND CHANCES

NEW JOURNEY

Walls down, no ammo or defenses
young and wild, we were addicted.
Falling in love with loving you.
No one will know
that you're here often,
that you have a spot in my dresser.
You'll be my best kept secret.

Stop comparing the love you knew
to the love you may currently have
nor to the one you'll have, the one you deserve.
They say, no two loves are the same.
I can promise you,
when you meet that person you'll understand my words.

Do not compare their love.

SECOND CHANCES

WARNING

My love is loud
and I'm terrible at lying,
so if you're looking
for a quiet girl
with white lies
I am not the one for you.

J. SAUNDERS

Please be careful
my heart is not made of paper,
you cannot rip it and tape it back together.

SECOND CHANCES

He controlled me,
unable to break the imaginary chains.

                                      Your goals and dreams are never too big,
                                  don't you dare make them smaller because
                                        someone else cannot see your vision.

J. SAUNDERS

For anyone who has felt their future isn't in their hands.
For the ones who have been abused mentally, physically
and sexually.
For the individuals who suffer from anxiety or depression,
I need you to know,
you do not need to be perfect.
You cannot help who you have trusted, and they let you down.
You will be more than okay
once you let out all of the pain you're holding onto.
It's not easy, I will not lie to you.
It'll hurt, and you'll feel so far within yourself
that you're unsure how to climb out
but you will.
For anyone who feels like they are suffering.
Remind yourself to breathe when your shoulders feel too heavy.
Let life into your soul.

SECOND CHANCES

Life is so much more than social media. You are not determined by your job or relationship status; your weight, height, skin colour, hair style, eye colour, the car you drive, designer shoes or $1 Old Navy flip flops. Waist trainers are not new, It's a redesigned "fitness" treatment from fashionable corsets during the French Revolution, throw them away. They're horrible for your body. Don't max out your credit card to keep up with the Joneses. Life is love, laughter, adventure and moments you usually don't capture on camera. Put the phone away. You cannot live life behind a device on an app while comparing yourself. When life is not based on the likes you have, It's based on the type of human you are. The story they'll share when you're gone. Life is the sunset you watch in silence with the people who love you just the way you are. Remain genuine.

I spent a chunk of my life living for someone else that I forgot what living for myself meant. I learned that lesson when the person I was living for, was no longer mine to live through.

Everything I knew, was no longer accessible to me.

What were the basic requirements to live for yourself? What do I wake up and do? My daily routine was just cancelled. How do I make a meal for one? What is it like to make myself happy, to love myself, to achieve a goal... for me?

I asked myself these questions every day, only to discover this was my chance to become a butterfly of my own. To love and create a life I enjoyed after enduring trauma and pain. Loss and suffering. There was hope. There is always hope. There is always a new beginning, a second chance and it's waiting for you when you're ready.

SECOND CHANCES

Poetry is not comfort.

It will not hold you and put you to bed at night
It's substance is temporary
Even the deepest purest love poem can keep you up
questioning the unknown

A poet is not sane

If they can write about love at its highest and give you
butterflies
Imagine how deep they can go with pain
pulling you down from within
Contradictions are easily spotted

J. SAUNDERS

You are worthy, deserving
You are amazing, wonderful
You are up and down, wild
You are open minded yet stubborn
Loving you is anything but easy
Dear self, I promise to never stop trying

SECOND CHANCES

Do you ever have this urge,
to get up,
run away and just be someone else?

I've been there,
and the best advice I can give someone,
is to spread your wings and be the best version of yourself.

Life isn't the movie X-Men.
No one is going to cut your wings,
unless you let them.

J. SAUNDERS

If you keep counting all the times you took a step back, you'll fail to see how many you had taken in the right direction.

DEAR WOMEN

When was the last time
you spent a night alone;
without your phone,
candles lit,
read a book,
ran a bath,
putting your fingers between your legs
learning all the ways
to love yourself?

Let them earn you.
Let them realize how good you are by staying true to yourself.
Allow yourself to grow and never apologize for it.
You are important just like anyone else.
Do not derail your happiness.
You always have a choice,
choose yourself,
without hesitation.

SECOND CHANCES

Until you learn to accept the past,
forgive yourself,
love your reflection,
have hope for the future,
you will always be suck
never moving forward.

J. SAUNDERS

Stop running away from yourself.
They won't make you happy.
Happiness starts and ends with you.
Self-love.

SECOND CHANCES

Love her for everything
she is and will become.
Support her dreams
even the wildest ones.
Hold her when she is sad,
the strong ones have moments too.
Lift her up when she is down,
for at times she is clumsy.
Be a man beyond anything,
she will give you the above and more.
Be the woman you need
and love you with all of her.

J. SAUNDERS

WHICH ROAD

You can keep looking back at past events and dwell on the things you cannot change.

Or

You can move on and ignore all the things that are not meant for you.

My motto:

Be a humble savage with a kind heart.

The best part about finding yourself
is knowing at the end of your journey,
there is love.

SECOND CHANCES

A sneak peek of "Love Notes" coming soon.

Love is

everything you will ever want and hate
all wrapped up into one emotional storm.

SECOND CHANCES

I write about love,
I believe in it
but I am by no means
ready to receive it.
I know that sounds like a contradiction
considering where it's coming from.
try to understand;
that love is a natural commitment,
and the last thing I want,
is for someone to love me,
the way I've loved someone else,
for all the right reasons
only to get nothing back in return.

J. SAUNDERS

CAN WE?

Can we start again? Can we meet again and leave our moment lost in the universe? Say our goodbyes there and save us the future heartache.

Can time be selfless and skip today? I'm selfish and my heart hurts thinking of you. Remembering the nights we let our love stay hidden instead of giving it to each other.

Can we start again? You're no longer within my arms. This is what I meant by future heartbreak.

Can we meet one day soon? So we can smile and laugh again? Enjoy the connection we never expected, just to leave what we could have had lost in that moment.

Can we start again?
I wasn't ready for this.

SECONDCHANCES

The impression you've left on me
isn't like the ink on my skin
but the new found colour in my soul
that beams through my grey image
whenever I write about you.

Like a black and white photo
that's been reprinted in colour.
You changed me.

I wanted him in ways no one could imagine.

His lips on my skin
his hands under my lace
his body between my hips.

I craved for him
like a cigarette pressed
in between my lips.

SECONDCHANCES

I've always wanted to love him beyond these sheets

                          Wanted and could are very far apart
                                Settling for another night
                              of less than what we should be
                                        because it's "him"
              However, even if I wanted the key to his heart
                                I refrained from asking
                      for the same reasons
                                  he never offered

This was us

I need to let you go
this I know
but my heart doesn't
it keeps asking me to stay.

Just one more minute;
one more hour,
one more day,
one more week.

Please stay,
I'm in love with him.

SECONDCHANCES

I fall
to love
Only to fall
and love again
To fall
Like nine lives of L
                    O
                        V
                            E
I faulter and fall each time

YOU'RE HERE TO STAY

What I'm about to say is rather selfish, but as a woman who has been through nothing except mayhem in life and with men; I keep you around because I find it rather comforting in your ability to quiet my mind, no matter the time.

SECOND CHANCES

I want you to be my last love
I was told, it lasts a lifetime

J.SAUNDERS

I wrote you countless messages.
They're all saved in a file on my phone.
I lacked bravery in sending them.
Your goodnights always had a hint of goodbye.
Envious of your ability to detach
as I fell more and more into you,
so I began writing you notes.
I knew I'd never send.
Some of them were blissful and empowering.
Some lustful and terrifyingly demanding of you.
Others were lonely and sad.
The complexity my heart and mind went through
will never be able to be deemed sane.
With you I was free
and you took me as I am.
Inspiring and empowering me.
We were wild.
So close, yet so far from love.
When my heart gets tired
and my mind is quiet,
sometimes I read all the words
from beginning to end
because it's the story
of how I fell in love with you
and why I never said, goodbye.

SECONDCHANCES

Love is graceful
I am not.
I have no comprehension
of moderation and time.
I am bold and overwhelming,
loud with passion.

I am one of those people
who love with all of me,
not pieces and fragments.
I've never believed
only half a heart could love.

I too understand
that love can be simple,
like someone taking you by the hand
and never letting go.

I am not graceful
but loving you is.

LOVE NOTE

I cannot remember
the last time
I got more than
four hours of sleep
and you not on my mind,
for the other 20 hours
I am awake for.

SECONDCHANCES

MR. WHO TOOK MY BREATH AWAY

My nights consisted of red wine,
ranting rambles called poetry
and Frank Sinatra heavily on replay.

Bleeding ears,
drunk tears
and vulgar words.

This was my way of getting over you.

ANOTHER LETTER TO HIM, ABOUT HIM

I wouldn't be able to tell you the moment it happened. The splitting second my heart fell and shattered into a million pieces over a man I was only infatuated with. The time when I found myself standing across the room from him with this gaze, starting from my shoes to my eyes. In that same minute, I was staring right back at him. Our eyes met in such perfection, the memories I forced away blinded me with pain and pleasure no one could ever explain. I never wanted someone with such intensity since the last time him and I were together. But what I can tell you is how I stood exactly in the same place for over 5 minutes before my girlfriend interrupted the gaze held between us. As she turned my body and moved me to the other side of the room, I felt his eyes on me. He followed my every move, just watching me and following my motions, until he matched with my steps. Lingering in the corner, I longed for his body standing over me. Instead I turned away in hopes of a distraction. I'd be lying to more than just myself if I didn't announce the way my inner body was screaming as every emotion I ever hid was displayed all over me. The way I felt my heart shatter over a year ago. The twists and turns in my gut. This overwhelming sense of pleasure I couldn't shake. I missed him. Every inch of him.

I WANT HIM

He didn't feel like butterflies
or a zoo.
He didn't make me feel insecure
or uncertain.
He didn't make me want to be
someone I wasn't.
He made me want to ask questions,
go against the grain of how I live
and step outside the lines of ordinary.
He was everything I was looking for
but couldn't keep.
He was a wild one.
The type that
impacted souls and broke hearts
while leaving you inspired,
ready to take on the world.

*Him. The one you compare to every other man
because he made you feel alive.*

www.ingramcontent.com/pod-product-compliance
Lightning Source LLC
Chambersburg PA
CBHW032023290426
44110CB00012B/640